Squash Rackets

Published in collaboration with the
SQUASH RACKETS ASSOCIATION

EP Publishing Limited

ISBN 0 7158 0217 8 (limp); 0 7158 0345 X (hard)

CONTENTS

FOREWORD

The growth of Squash Rackets continues unabated on account both of the characteristics of the game and because it is easy to learn and enjoy.

The total of people – very young, middle aged and older – who take it up and wish to learn quickly is innumerable. On its own this little book is ideal as a teaching guide and refresher, and as a back-up to tuition it is unbeatable.

The Squash Rackets Association is delighted to be involved in the updating and improvement of this little work; I, as my predecessors, can recommend you all to use it for your greater enjoyment of the game.

Roderic Phillips.

Major-General A. R. Fyler C.B., OBE.
Former President,
Squash Rackets Association

3

INTRODUCTION

Squash rackets is growing at a remarkably rapid rate, not only because it is fun, induces competitiveness, aids fitness and stimulates social activity - but also because those that try it find it easy to learn.

However, whether novice or player with some knowledge, to get more fun and more value from, and to become more proficient at the game, some guidance and advice is advisable - indeed necessary. The best form of this is, of course, individual coaching; however there are very few professionals and it will be some time before there are sufficient qualified coaches to meet the demand in schools, clubs and sports centres.

This book is highly significant and necessary on two counts. It will help fill the gap until coaching for all is more readily available and it will complement the coaching given on courses. The book is progressive in its approach - the best value from it initially will come from step by step study and practice.

It does not take very long for enthusiastic players to become competent - provided they keep on the right lines - and be able to play for their club or even county.

The advice on play in this book was written by the late Sam Jagger who coached squash at Lancing College for twenty-seven years. He produced such a stream of good players that Lancing Old Boys won the Londonderry Cup (the Tournament for the Old Boys of all schools) seventeen times between 1948 and 1971.

HISTORY OF THE GAME

Squash rackets is said to have started at Harrow School over a hundred years ago. Growth at first was slow in this country and up to 1914, courts were to be found mainly in country houses and were as varied in size as were the balls in pace. The Tennis and Rackets Association on its foundation in 1907, appointed a sub-committee to draw up a code of rules, but it was not until 1928 that squash had its own association, nor until the thirties that there was a growing number of purely squash clubs being formed all over the country. The Services, particularly the R.A.F., were quick to recognise the benefits of this game, and even before the last war most R.A.F. stations had at least one squash court. Many Service establishments now have their own court or courts.

In recent years the growth has seen the spread of the game broaden from its original base of public school and clubs, whose members had such a background, to grammar schools and to wider social levels. It became accepted practice for new universities to incorporate squash courts in their planning. The public authorities are increasingly becoming aware not only of the benefits of the game to their ratepayers, but importantly, the commercial viability of squash in any sports or leisure centre in which courts may be hired. This commercial viability has had a further far reaching effect - the establishment of a large number of clubs and centres under a single organisation. It is in the area of Public

Courts, the provision of courts in education authority schools as an accepted principle, and commercial developments that the greatest growth significance lies over the next few years.

The provision of facilities for members and spectators is improving rapidly; the development of the glass back wall is singularly significant. It is now possible to televise and film squash, thus opening up the game to many thousands in their homes who have never heard of it. Training films, and films of leading players in match play have increased the understanding of the game and its popularity.

A strong central organisation is required to cope with the many problems arising out of a game which is now played in over 60 countries in all parts of the world. Two interesting examples of this growth are the proposals in Japan to build 7,000 courts in five years and the building of over 400 in Mexico in 18 months. In this country there are some 200 known projects for building new courts. Until 1966 all these international duties were performed by the Squash Rackets Association. In that year, an International Squash Rackets Federation was formed which has relieved the S.R.A. of some of its international obligations.

Europe, with major developments in Sweden and Holland, is poised on the edge of even more rapid expansion. The European championships are now annual events and the formation of the European Federation marks a great advance. Germany in particular is building a very large number of courts.

The Squash Rackets Association was founded in 1928 to take over the administration of the game from the Tennis and Rackets Association. Starting with a membership of 25 clubs it has grown so that there are now over 1,500 affiliated clubs in England alone, while there are far more than that number abroad affiliated to the S.R.A. either directly or through their national associations. The game is controlled by a council on which the clubs are represented through their county and area associations. The Services, the Universities and the Women's Squash Rackets Association and many overseas associations also have their representatives on this council, as have also the 3,500 individual and junior members of the S.R.A. The association can therefore lay claim to be a completely democratic body.

The game is also played in the U.S.A. and Canada; but it is played in a different court with different equipment and different scoring. This makes serious competition between players of either type of game difficult and truly world wide events not yet practicable.

THE GAME OF SQUASH RACKETS

The game of squash rackets is played between two players (singles) or two pairs of players (doubles). The doubles game, which really requires a larger court, is now played in England in singles courts, although there are plans to rebuild a number of the full sized doubles courts.

The ball is served by one player, from a service box, on to the front wall above the cut line, so that on its rebound it falls into the opposite back quarter of the court bounded by the half-court line and the short line.

The server is known as "Hand-in" and the receiver as "Hand-out".

Hand-out may then either (a) volley the ball or (b) hit the ball after it has bounced once on the floor. In either case, he plays the ball to the front wall either (a) directly or (b) by way of a side or back wall, and the server then receives and returns it similarly. Play goes on until a player fails to make a good return, when his opponent scores a point (if hand-in) or takes over the service (if hand-out).

It is important to note that only the server can score points. A return is "good" so long as

(a)   the ball remains within the boundaries of the court,

(b)   the ball hits the front wall above the tin before it touches the floor.

(c)   the ball does not bounce on the floor more than once before it is returned.

A marker controls matches, but usually a referee is appointed as well. The latter is in overall control and makes all decisions covering lets, the award of points and appeals against calls of the marker by either player. Where there is only one official he must act in both capacities.

Dress

The usual dress for men is white shorts, white canvas shoes (with soles not black, otherwise the court will be marked) and a white short-sleeved shirt. For women, a white blouse or shirt with short white skirt or shorts.

The Court

The walls of the court should be white or near white. The size of the court is standard and all floor and wall dimensions are measured from the junction of the floor and walls. Lines are painted red and should be two inches (5.0 cm) wide, whether on the floor or walls of the court. The "Tin" consists of a plywood or metal sheet extending right across the front wall, surmounted by a two-inch strip of wood, known as the board, painted red, as shown. The height to the top of this board is nineteen inches (48.3 cm) from the floor.

A court will have some 12 electric lights or fluorescent strips suspended above the court.

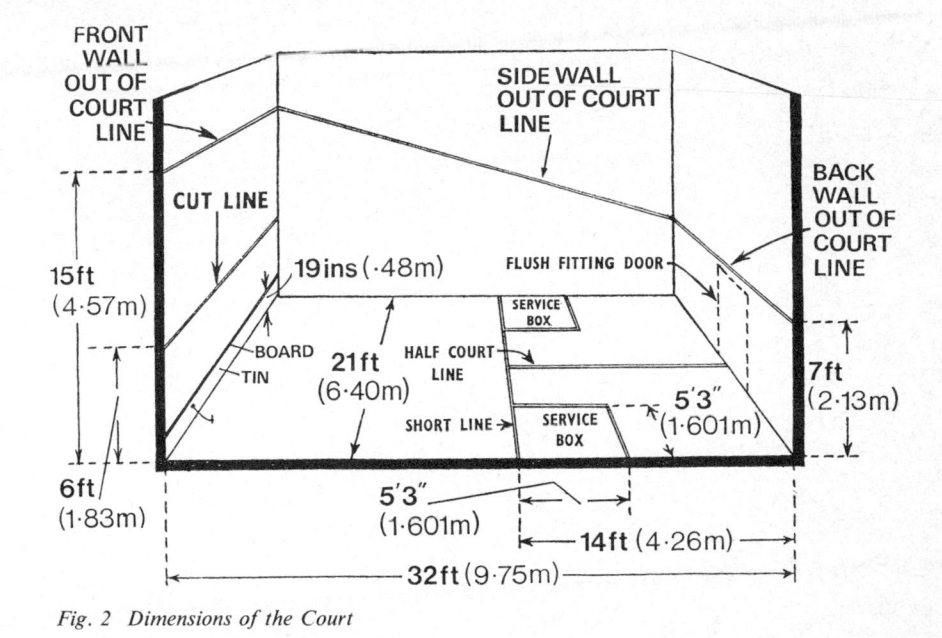

Fig. 1 Suitable Dress

FRONT WALL OUT OF COURT LINE

SIDE WALL OUT OF COURT LINE

BACK WALL OUT OF COURT LINE

CUT LINE

19 ins (·48m)

FLUSH FITTING DOOR

SERVICE BOX

15ft (4·57m)

BOARD
TIN

21ft (6·40m)

HALF COURT LINE

SHORT LINE

SERVICE BOX

5'3" (1·601m)

7ft (2·13m)

6ft (1·83m)

5'3" (1·601m)

14ft (4·26m)

32ft (9·75m)

Fig. 2 Dimensions of the Court

The Racket

The framework of the head of the racket is of wood and strung with gut, nylon or similar material. The handle shaft may be of wood, cane, metal or glass fibre. There may be some "whip" in the shaft and the grip may be of any suitable material - e.g., leather, rubber or towelling. The towel grip is very popular as it helps to absorb perspiration. No weight is specified, as the most suitable is usually chosen by "feel", but the dimensions of the racket shown opposite are maximum and should not be exceeded.

The Ball

The rubber ball is small and round with an even matt surface and finish. It is obtainable in varying speeds to suit the court on which the game is being played. These speeds are indicated by a coloured dot: Yellow (very slow), White (slow), Red (medium) and Blue (fast).

The size is shown in the illustration opposite and it should be from between 23.3 grm and 24.6 grm in weight. Balls must pass the testing committee of the Squash Rackets Association and, if they comply with the specifications laid down, they may bear the standard S.R.A. mark.

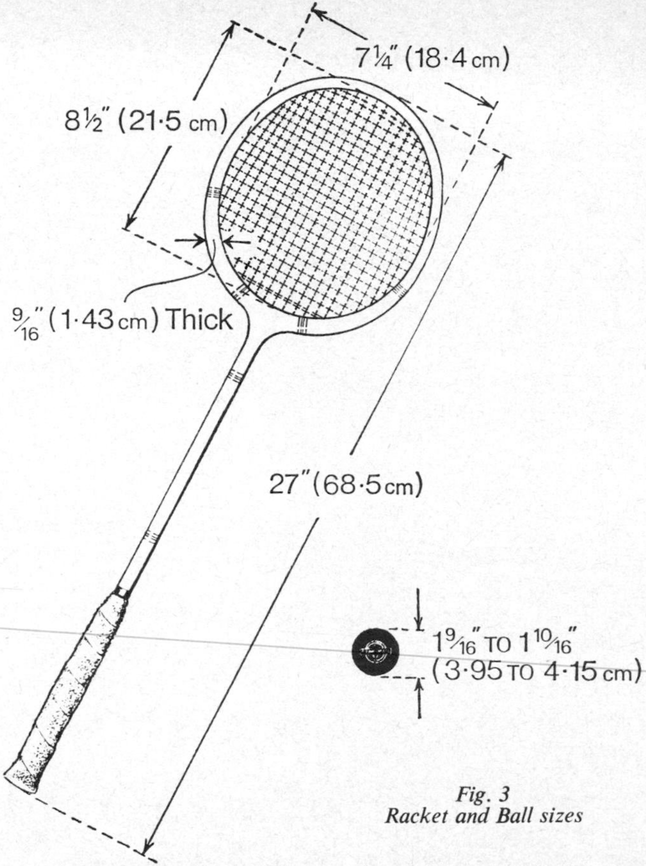

7¼" (18·4 cm)

8½" (21·5 cm)

$\frac{9}{16}$" (1·43 cm) Thick

27" (68·5 cm)

$1\frac{9}{16}$" TO $1\frac{10}{16}$" (3·95 TO 4·15 cm)

Fig. 3
Racket and Ball sizes

8

THE SINGLES GAME

The right to serve first is decided by the spin of a racket and the server may serve from either service box.

X wins the toss and serves. Y returns the ball and from then it is struck alternately until X either wins a point or loses the service. X continues to score points as long as he continues to win rallies while serving. If X puts the ball out of court, into the tin or board, serves a double fault or is beaten by Y's return, Y then becomes the server and so on throughout the match.

For the initial service of each game or "hand" the server may serve from either box, but after scoring a point he serves from the other box and then from each box alternately as long as he remains hand-in.

If hand-in serves from the wrong box and his opponent takes the service, there is no penalty and the service counts as if it had been made from the correct box. His opponent may demand the service to be re-taken from the correct box, provided he has not taken the service. Points are scored by hand-in when his opponent fails to make a good return.

Only hand-in may score points.

Fig. 4 The Service

9

Fig. 5 Correct Service

The Service

If hand-in serves from the right-hand service box, he may take up the position shown in Fig. 5, ready to deliver a forehand service. The backhand stroke may also be used from this service box.

A service from the left-hand court may also be served either forehand or backhand but in both cases the following points must be observed for the correct service:

(a)   Stand with one foot or both feet touching the floor within the service box.

(b)   Throw the ball from the hand into the air.

(c)   Serve the ball on to the front wall above the cut line so that on its return, unless volleyed, it would fall on the floor in the quarter court nearest the back wall and opposite to the service box from which the service has been delivered.

Service Faults

Note: Any combination of faults in the one service constitutes only one fault.

1.   It is a foot-fault unless the server has at least one foot in contact with the floor, within the service box, at the moment of striking the ball; no part of this qualifying foot may be touching a line, the wall or the floor outside the box, though the other foot may be anywhere inside or outside the box. (*see fig.* 6).

2.   It is a fault if the ball is served on to the front wall on or below the "cut" line, but above the tin and board. (*see fig.* 7).

Fig. 6 **Service Faults** *Fig. 7*

Fig. 8

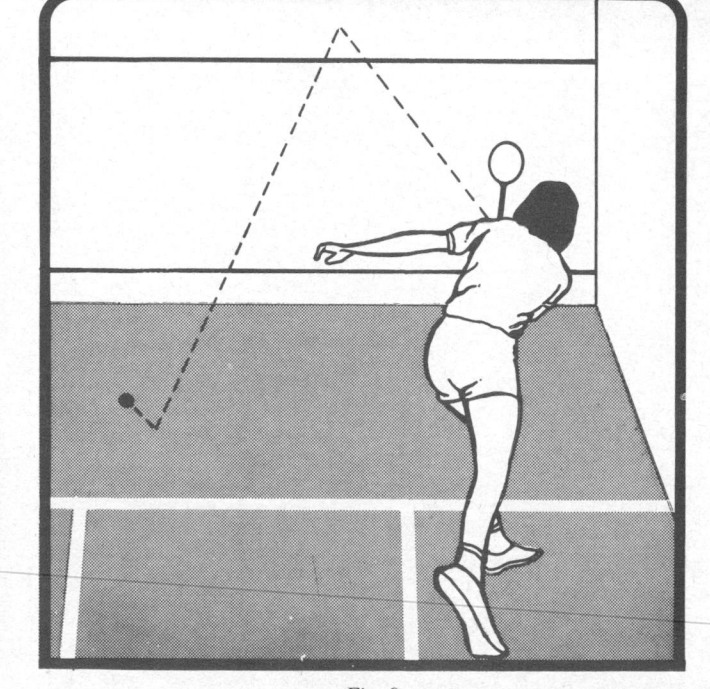

Fig. 9

3. It is a "fault" if the ball first touches the floor on the half-court line or in the half court from which the service is delivered.

4. It is a "fault" if the ball first touches the floor on or in front of the short line, *i.e.*, if it drops short of the service court.

Hand-out may, if he chooses, take a fault and the service becomes good. If hand-out takes a fault and returns the ball down or out of court, hand-in wins the point. If hand-out does not take the fault, the ball ceases to be in play when it has bounced twice upon the floor.

If the ball touches the server or anything he wears or carries before it has bounced twice, the server loses the stroke.

Hand-out does not need to say anything and should not do so. He accepts the service by playing a shot, and does not accept it by refraining from doing so.

Serving Hand-out

Server serves his hand-out and loses the stroke:

(a)   If he fails to hit the ball correctly or the ball does not at least carry to the front wall above the tin.

(b)   If he serves the ball out of court.

(c)   If the ball strikes another wall before the front wall.

(d)   If he serves two consecutive faults.

Appeals to Referee

Hand-in may not appeal against the Marker's call of "Fault" or "Footfault" to his first service. He may appeal against all other calls, which would result in his losing the right to serve, i.e. services called "Not up" or "Out" or calls of "Fault" or "Footfault" to his second service. Hand-out may appeal against the Marker's failure to call "Fault", "Footfault", "Not up" or "Out", but in the case of faults must not take that service, if he wishes to appeal, as by doing so, he would be making the alleged fault good anyway. In the other cases, he should play the ball and only appeal if he loses the subsequent rally. After delivery of a service no appeal may be made for anything that occurred before that service was delivered.

RETURN AND SUBSEQUENT PLAY

After the first service is delivered, play should be continuous as far as possible. Bad light or other circumstances beyond the players' control may stop play. If play is resumed the same day, the match shall continue at the score as it was when play ceased, but if it is resumed the next or a subsequent day, the match shall be started afresh unless both players agree to continue with the score as it was when play closed.

Good Return

A return is good if the ball, before it has bounced twice on the floor, is returned by the striker on to the front wall above the board, without touching the floor or any part of the strikers' body or clothing, provided the ball is not hit twice or out of court.

Winning Strokes

A player wins a stroke:

(a)   When his opponent serves his hand-out.

(b)   If his opponent fails to make a good return of the ball in play.

(c)   If the ball touches the striker's opponent or anything he wears or carries, except in those cases otherwise provided for under "obstructions."

A winning stroke by hand-in scores a point.

A winning stroke by hand-out gives him the service.

Fig. 10
Player on left loses stroke

SCORING

A match consists of the best of five games, each game being of nine up. The player first winning nine points wins the game, except that, if the score is called eight-all for the first time, hand-out may, if he chooses, before the next service is delivered, set the game to two. In this case, the player who first scores two points wins the game.

These two points do not have to be scored consecutively. Hand-out must in either case clearly indicate his choice to the marker, if any, and to his opponent, by saying either "No Set" or "Set Two".

The score does not go beyond ten. Thus, in the case of "No Set" one player will win the game 9-8, and in the case of "Set Two" one player will win it 10-9 or 10-8.

The Marker

The game is controlled by the marker, who calls the play and score. The server's score is called first.

If during play the marker calls "Not-up" or "Out", the rally must stop and if his decision is altered on appeal a "let" is allowed, unless the Referee decrees that the Marker has called "Not-up" or "Out" to an undoubted winning shot, which was in fact correct, in which case he may award the stroke accordingly.

When no referee is appointed the marker exercises all the powers of the referee.

Referees

A referee may be appointed and, if so, all appeals are directed to him.

The decision of the referee is final.

Let and when allowed

A let is an undecided stroke, and the service or rally in respect of which a let is allowed does not count and the service is taken again from the same box. However, a let does not annul a previous fault.

KEEPING OUT OF OPPONENT'S WAY

A player must do all he can to give his opponent a clear and fair view of the ball in play and give him room to play his stroke. A player must always leave his opponent as far as possible free to play the ball to any part of the front wall or to either side wall near the front wall.

If in the opinion of the referee there is unnecessary interference with the striker, "stop" is called. Play stops at once and a stroke is awarded to the player interfered with.

Unnecessary crowding constitutes obstruction, even if the player is not actually prevented from reaching or playing the ball.

Fig. 11
Player on the right loses stroke, unnecessary obstruction

IS IT A LET OR A POINT?

Fig. 12

Fig. 13

If a fair ball, after hitting the front wall and before being played again, touches a player or anything he wears or carries before touching the floor twice, the touched player loses the stroke.

If a ball is struck as a good return and it hits the striker's opponent or anything he wears or carries before it reaches the front wall, it is a point to the striker if the ball would have reached the front wall directly, unless the striker has "turned" on the ball, or has already played and missed.

Fig. 14

If a ball is struck as a good return, but would have hit either side wall first, it is a let. Similarly if a good return has already hit the side wall on its way to the front wall, it is also a let, unless an undoubted winning shot has been intercepted, in which case a stroke is awarded.

Fig. 15

If a ball would not have made a good return, the striker shall lose the stroke. For other cases in which a let is allowed see Rule 18, page 47.

ADVICE ON PLAY

The Grip

The grip shown is the orthodox one. Many players have developed their own variations on this, and provided a player has a grip which is comfortable and enables him to play the full range of forehand and backhand strokes successfully, then that particular grip is correct for him.

Do not grip the racket tightly. Every muscle of your body should be relaxed when you position yourself ready to strike the ball. This is even true of the fingers that grip the racket. Only when you strike the ball does your grip tighten.

The Swing of the Racket

Points to note are:

(a) your body movement is like playing forward at cricket.

(b) the racket moves nearly in a semi-circle (Figs. 18, 19 and 20).

Fig. 16 The Grip

To guide you when practising this swing, place a hearth-rug in a suitable position so that its long edge can be used to check the straight-line movement of the racket head. Stand a racket's length away from one of the sides of it, with your feet a comfortable distance apart.

Now swing the racket. The handle of it should go up as far as your right shoulder and when you follow through after you have struck the imaginary ball, the racket continues along the line of the edge of the rug.

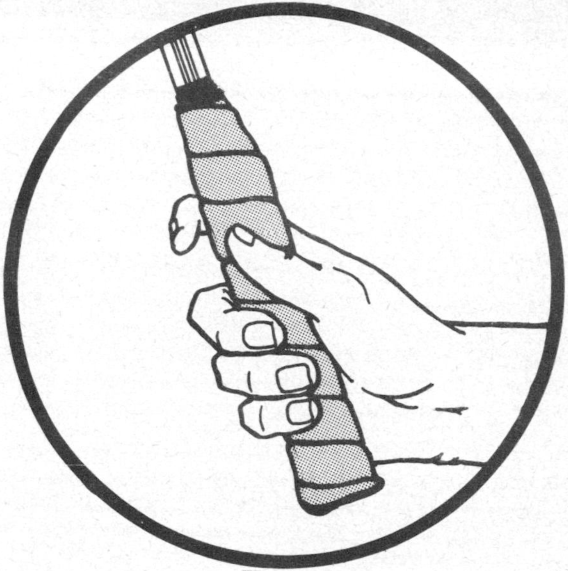

(c) Use your wrist when you strike the ball, bend your knees a little and lean forward slightly. The whole movement is very similar to that used by a person throwing a flat stone into the sea so that it skims along the water.

It is well to realise, however, that most modern aggressive players cock their wrist at the top of the back swing as shown in Fig. 17.

18

Try this and you will find what added power it will give you. So if you want to hit the ball harder or to cut the ball, you should learn the "cocked-wrist" back lift, but remember that your margin of error is greatly widened by its use and unless you are a fairly competent player, you will be liable to make more errors and to lose accuracy.

Always remember that you have your opponent in the same court and the player with the exaggerated back swing or follow through is obstructive and dangerous, and may be penalised. The top players obtain their power from timing and correct use of the wrist, not by wild swinging of the racket.

Striking the ball from three positions

Remember that you should be properly balanced when you strike the ball, with your weight evenly distributed on both feet. Watch the ball right on to your racket. Then immediately you have struck it, go up on your toes and you are ready to move into the middle of the court again.

To be a good player, you must take endless trouble to be sure that you can strike the ball correctly, early or very late as the strategy of the game requires.

Fig. 17
The alternative position for the back lift. (Compare with Fig. 18)

1. Just after the top of its bounce (Fig. 21). This is the usual position of striking the ball when it is just starting to descend. Keep as far away from it as you can. Do not hurry too much but wait for the ball to reach the top of its bounce. Practise hard to strike the ball like this.

19

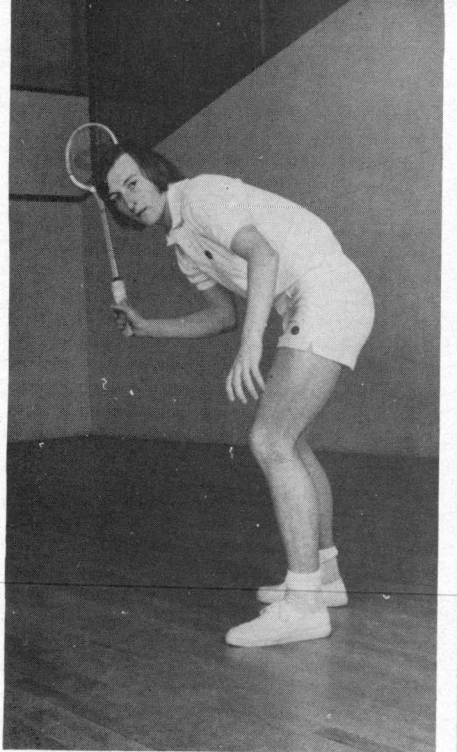

Fig. 18   *Back lift*   Fig. 19   *Striking position*   Fig. 20   *Follow-through*

Fig. 21 The usual position when the ball is struck just after the top of its bounce

Fig. 22 Striking the ball early

Fig. 23 Striking the ball very late

2. Before it reaches the top of its bounce. As the ball approaches you, go to meet it and hit it, but stand well away from it. You will find that if you wish to speed up the game you will have to take the ball early, as in Fig. 22.

3. Very late. Learn to hit the ball when it is about a foot or less from the ground. Obviously to do this you must keep well back from it as it approaches you (Fig. 23).

Sometimes you will find that your opponent is in position in the centre of the court and if you take the ball too late he will be on his heels by the time you strike it. Taking the ball late is often the best way of masking your stroke.

Keeping the Racket Head Up

When you are waiting for your opponent to strike the ball the head of your racket should be "up" and the racket across your body in front of you (Fig. 24).

When you take your racket back before a forehand or a backhand stroke, the wrist should be cocked so that the head of your racket will be "up".

Always aim to keep the head of your racket as far "up" as you can when you strike the ball. To put this another way: always aim to keep the head of the racket "up" relative to the direction of your forearm, as this is the strongest position of the wrist.

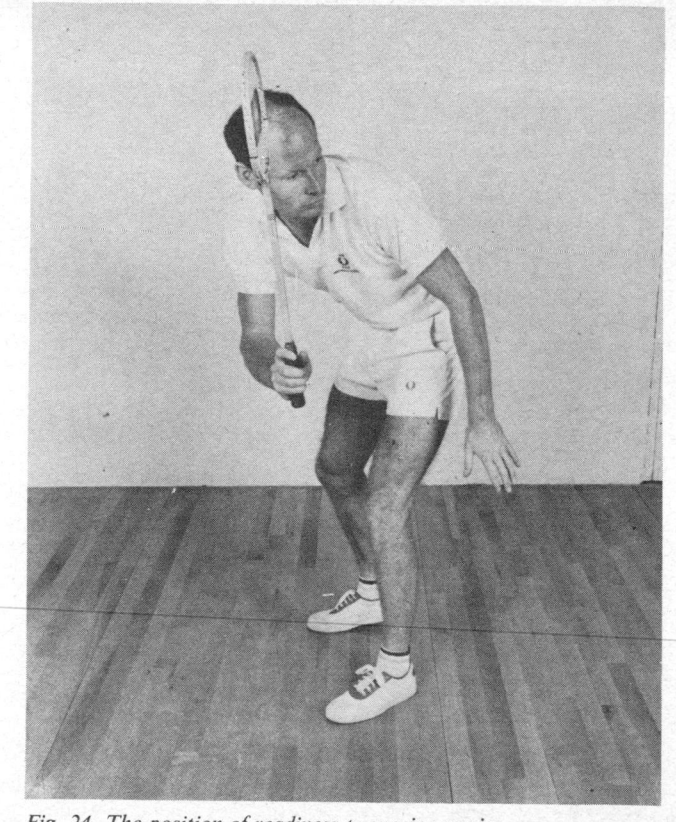

Fig. 24 The position of readiness to receive service

Taking the ball off the back wall

When taking the ball off the back wall, you must turn round to face the back wall or even the opposite side wall with your racket held back ready to strike the ball, but keep as far away from the ball as you can.

If you study the pictures, you will be able to see the correct positions of the feet and the body for such strokes.

Fig. 25 The ball that comes far enough from the wall to return normally.

Fig. 26 The ball that does not rebound far enough from the back wall to allow a normal swing.

A player need never be beaten except by the ball that drops really dead or clings to the back wall.

Use the side walls to get up the most difficult ones and hit upwards and hit hard.

The higher the ball arrives on to the front wall off the side wall, the more time there is for you to get to the centre of the court, and once there, you can almost certainly return the next stroke of your opponent.

The two regular returns for balls coming off the back wall are:

(a)   a return up the nearer side wall to a ball that has rebounded far enough to allow a normal strike.

(b)   a boast for the very difficult one (Fig. 28).

Do not boast the ball unnecessarily, as it is apt to give your opponent an easy shot in the front of the court but do not try to play the straight return down the side wall if there is any danger of hitting the back wall with your racket as you play the shot.

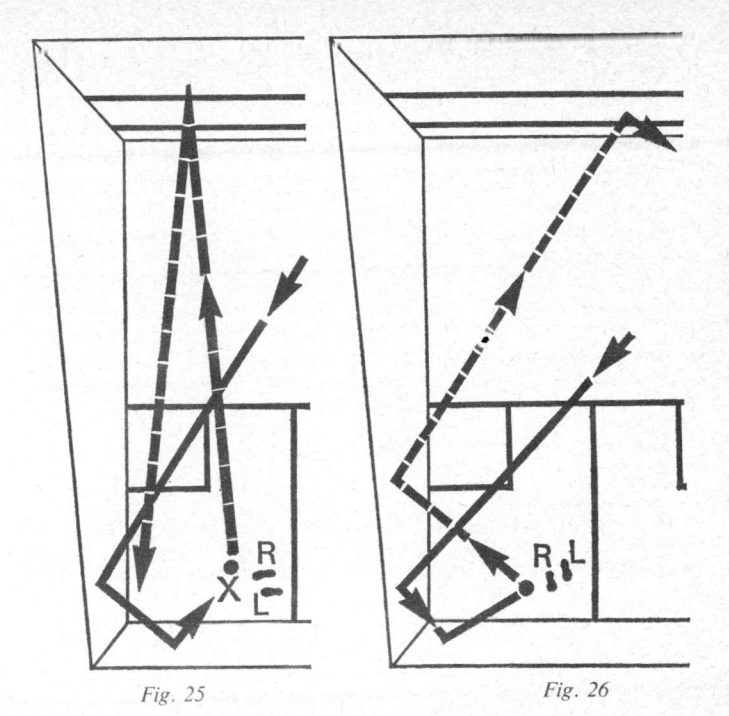

Fig. 25   *Fig. 26*

The two returns most often used for balls coming off the back wall. In Fig. 26 the ball should be hit hard and upwards

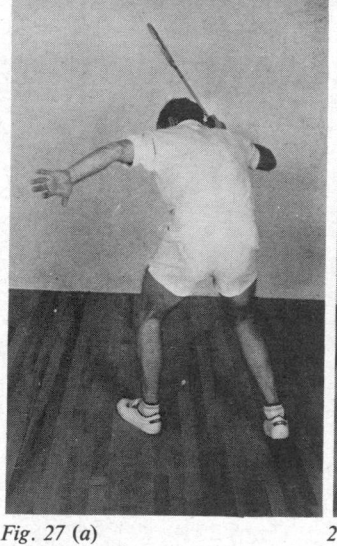
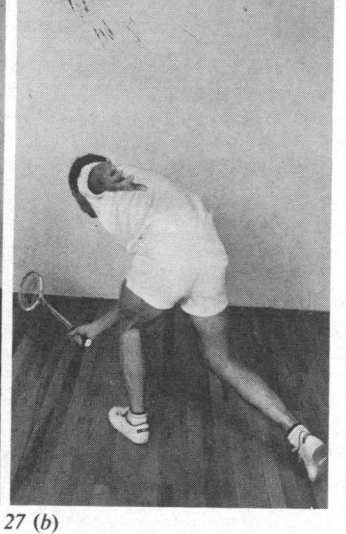
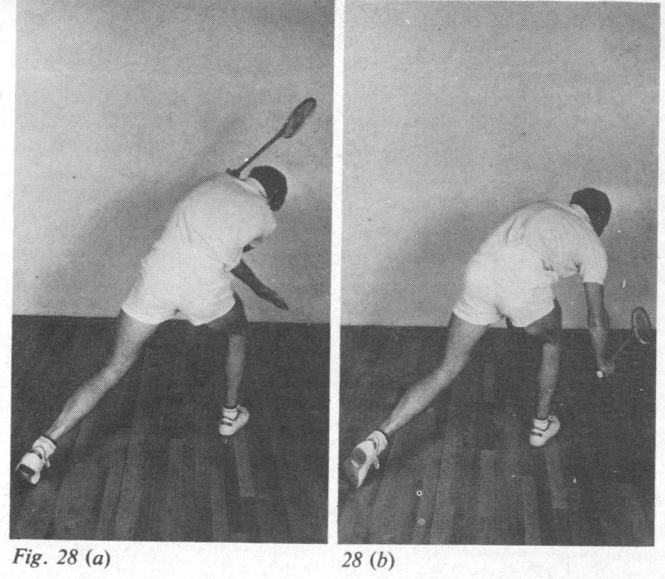

Fig. 27 (a)   27 (b)   Fig. 28 (a)   28 (b)

A ball that hits the back wall fairly hard and rebounds well clear of it may give an opening for a wide range of shots, such as the drop shot to either front corner or the reverse angle.

It is not always necessary to be on the defensive when your opponent's shot goes to the back of the court.

Figs. 27 and 28 show the correct positions for commencement of stroke to retrieve ball from back corner. Note Figs. 27a and 28a where body is placed to enable full swing of racket to be taken clear of back wall. In Figs. 27b and 28b swing continues prior to hitting ball well to the side of the body with a view to hitting it high and hard, and as far forward as possible on the side wall. Note that the knees are bent to make sure of getting under the ball.

24

1. Watch your opponent strike the ball

Watch your opponent strike the ball and then immediately move off in the direction in which he has struck it. If you are very fast on your feet you can almost overtake the ball! Many people watch only the front wall or they only watch the ball until it is nearing their opponent and then they watch the front wall. Fig. 29 is correct

Fig. 29 The player on the right is in the correct position, watching his opponent strike the ball

Fig. 30 The INCORRECT position

Fig. 31

The centre court position – watching opponent retrieve ball from backhand corner of court

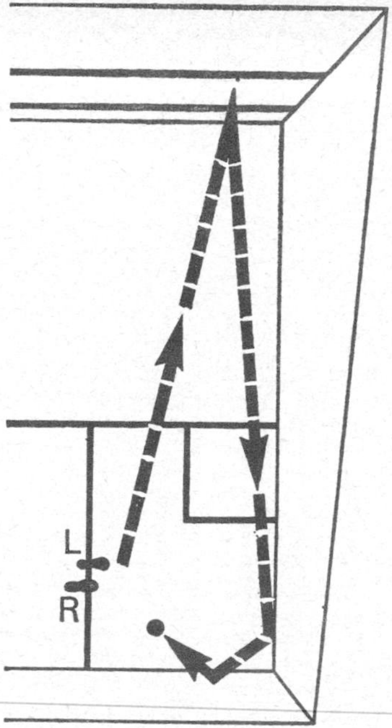

Fig. 32

A length up a side wall (forehand) hit hard

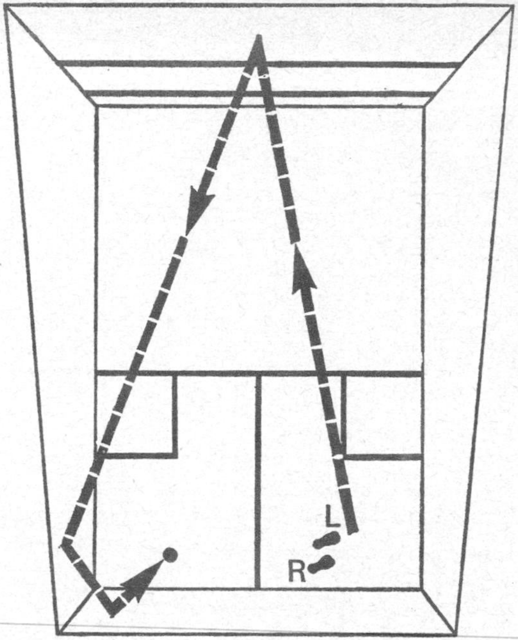

Fig. 33

A length up and over to the opposite corner (backhand), hit softly. Note where the ball strikes the front wall.

except that the player should be on his toes ready to move in any direction, as in Fig. 31. Fig. 30 is incorrect.

Be quite sure that you are watching the ball right on to your opponent's racket. Ask a friend to stand in the court balcony and tell you if you are really watching your opponent striking the ball and if you are immediately moving off in the direction in which he has struck it.

2. Regain the centre court position

The actual centre of the court is clearly marked by two red lines which meet there and is therefore known as the "T." If the ball is a slow one, the centre-court position is actually on the "T" line. If the ball is fast, the centre-court position is two or three feet further back.

As soon as you have struck the ball when you are serving, move very quickly and take up your place as shown in Fig. 31. Notice the position of the head and of the feet. You are almost facing the side wall. You must be slightly on your toes and your knees must be slightly bent so that you can move off quickly in any direction.

3. Hitting to a length

All courts are different and whenever you start a match, try in the first game to get a length.

A length means that when you hit the ball up and down the side walls or across the court to the opposite back corner, it will be very difficult for your opponent to get it up if he allows it to reach the back of the court.

Remember that you can hit a ball hard and to a length (Fig. 32) but you can also hit it softly and to a length. If you wish to get a length with a softly hit ball, you must hit it higher up on the front wall (Fig. 33).

4. Hitting the ball into the back corners

The foundation of the game is to go on hitting the ball up the side walls or across the court into the opposite corner until you get such a good length ball into the back corner that your opponent is in difficulties. If he is a very good player he will return this difficult ball, but not to a length, and then you are in an attacking position so that you can play a drop shot or an angle shot or some other stroke that may possibly win the point.

Very often among the moderate club players and below the difficult length ball into the back corner is a winner.

Do not be in too much of a hurry to attempt a winning stroke. Rather let it be your aim to hit the ball into the back corners until you can gain a winning position in the front half of the court.

Do not take up the position shown in Fig. 30 because the head is facing the front wall and the tendency will be to look in the same direction. To watch your opponent strike the ball from this position is a most unnatural movement.

As soon as you have struck the ball when returning the service of your opponent, bound into the centre of the court. And, finally, whenever you strike the ball during a rally, rush for the centre-court position as fast as you can, You MUST be there before your opponent strikes the ball. You must realise from this that it is essential to play a stroke which will cause your opponent to move from the "T" and give you a clear path to it.

THE SERVICE

The lob service is the best, provided the height of the court roof allows. It should be played from the front corner of the service box near the wall, and hit upwards on to the front wall, striking it about the centre of the area between the cut line and out of court line. The ball should continue upwards and strike the further side wall just below the out of court line, some three-quarters of the way down the court; and bounce on the floor before striking the back wall. Should the court have a low roof, or as a variety, the defensive service can be used. For this, strike the ball as close to the centre of the court as possible, so that it hits the front wall three-quarters of the way across and only a few feet above the cut line, with the aim of bringing the ball back close to the opposite side wall to a good length.

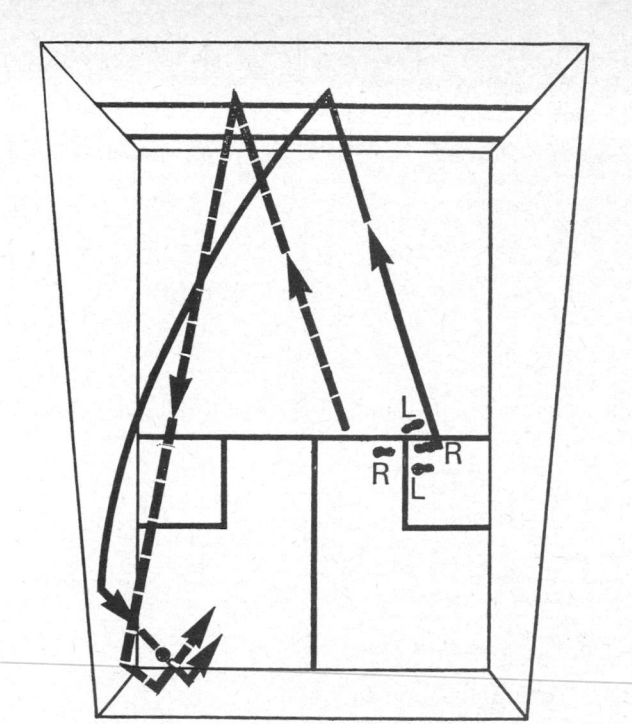

Fig. 34
Solid line: *the slow lob service*
Dotted line: *the backhand serve from the middle of the court*

28

THE RETURN OF SERVICE

As it is easier to move forwards than it is to move backwards, the striker should not get too close to the side wall (Fig. 35), and should remain fairly close to the back wall in order to be able to estimate more accurately whether the service will be a good length one, in which case the striker should move forward and take it early before it reaches the corner, or whether it will rebound for an easy return having hit the back wall fairly hard or high.

Suggested positions for hand-out to stand to await the service are shown in Fig. 35.

He should be on his toes, and as always, watching his opponent and not the front wall, in order to anticipate accurately the type and direction of the service and not be surprised by a sudden hard hit shot or one down the centre of the court.

There are three regular returns of service:

(a)   The striker can hit the ball up the side wall to a length (Fig. 36.)

(b)   The ball can be returned high to the opposite back corner of the court, taking care that the ball is played over the opponent's head, and not presenting him with an easy volley ball. (Fig. 37 – solid line.)

This return can be dangerous for, if the server is a good volleyer, he can kill an inaccurate shot with a volley just above the tin. Therefore practise a slow high length return over the server's head as he stands in the centre court position.

(c)   The striker can play a volley just above the tin in the front corner nearest to him. (Fig. 37 – dotted line.)

By concentrating only on these three returns of service you will, with patience, develop accuracy.

One final hint: you should volley the service as much as you can.

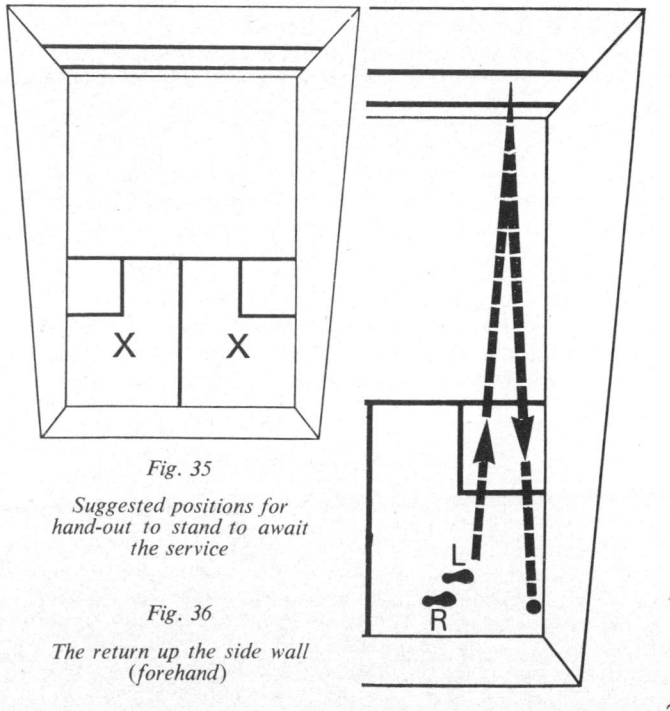

Fig. 35

*Suggested positions for
hand-out to stand to await
the service*

Fig. 36

*The return up the side wall
(forehand)*

THE CUT STROKES

These cut strokes can be played either on the forehand or the backhand.

In recent years the ball has changed and it is now possible to kill the slow ball from positions in front of

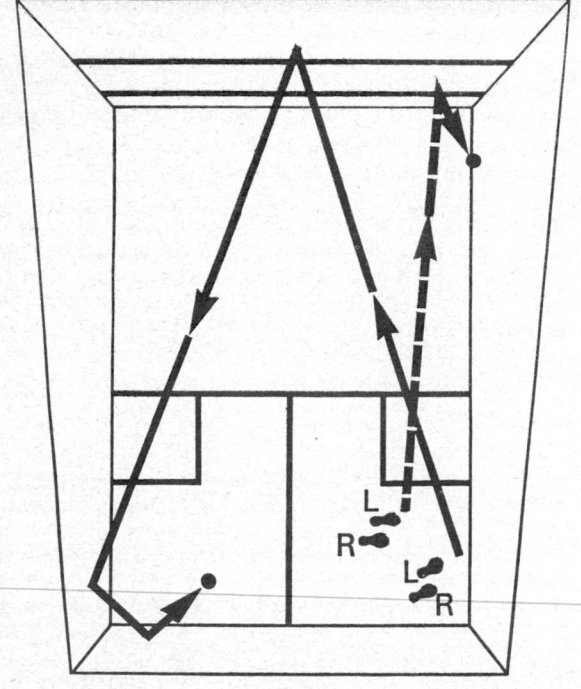

Fig. 37

Solid line: *the return to the opposite corner (forehand), hit high*
Dotted line: *the straight volley just above the tin (forehand)*

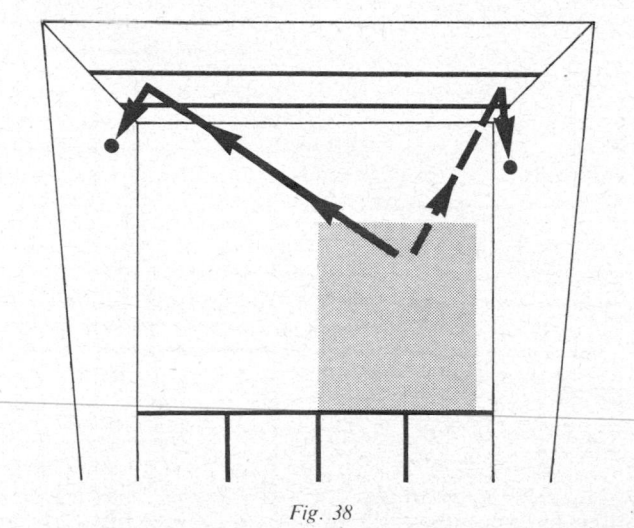

Fig. 38

The cut strokes played from the right-hand side of the court. The dotted line indicates the kill to the nearer wall and the solid line the shot played across court

the centre line of the court by taking the ball at the top of its bounce and by hitting it with cut and either with a great deal of power, or with a quick hard flick of the wrist. The ball should be hit as near as possible to the tin and it will be dead before it reaches the centre line of the court (Fig. 38).

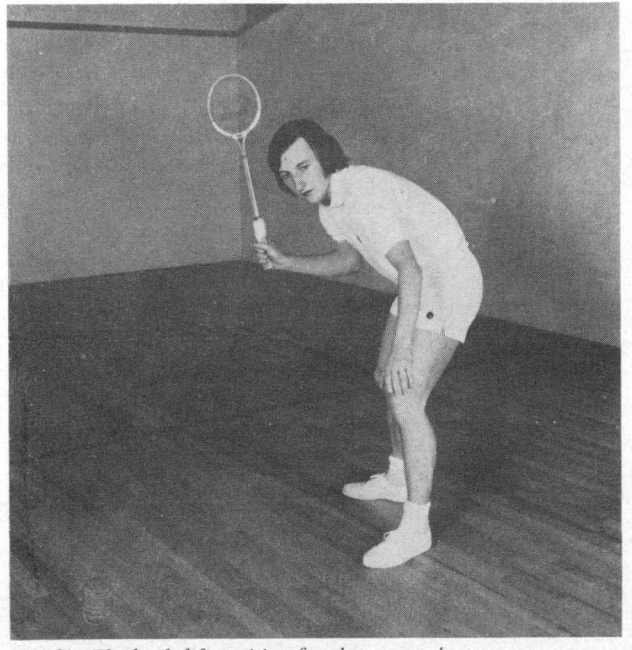

Fig. 39 shows the back lift position for the cut stroke.

This stroke can also be played so that the ball will nick on the side walls. The ball will strike the front wall about two feet above the tin (Fig. 40). Remember that the ball must be hit hard, and must also carry a good deal of cut.

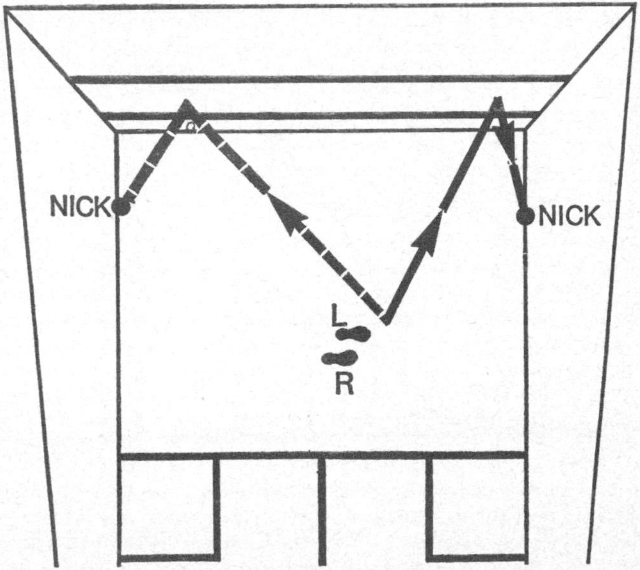

Fig. 39 The back lift position for the cut strokes

Fig. 40 Playing the shot so that it will nick on the side wall

THE DROP SHOT

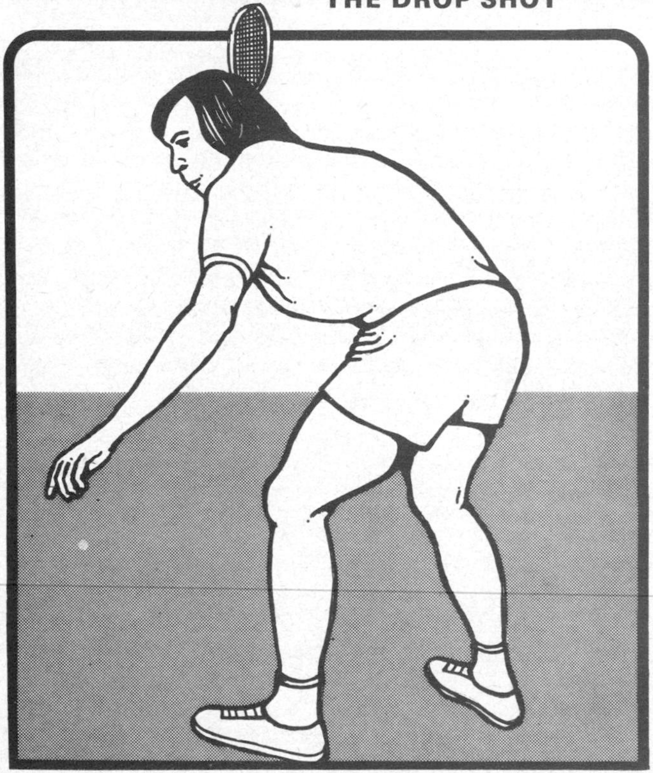

There are two drop shots and both should be learnt.

(*a*) Hit the ball early, just before it reaches the top of its bounce. You are, therefore, striking the ball from a position which is above the level of the tin. Hit it down-

Fig. 41
The drop shot (i) – back lift position

Fig. 42 *The drop shot (ii) – striking the ball*

wards with cut so that when it hits the front wall it will continue downwards (Figs. 41, 42 and 43). This is the easiest way to gain a nick on the side wall.

(b)   Keep well away from the ball and hit it very late, as near to the ground as possible (Fig. 44). The ball is hit after it has reached the top of its bounce. The advantage of this method, which is the usual one, is that your opponent has to wait behind you and he often finds himself on his heels and therefore unable to make the quick start that is necessary to reach the ball.

The best positions from which to play the drop shot are shown in Fig. 45.

You generally aim for a nick with your drop shot and you should hit the ball as softly as you can. When a drop shot is played from the front of the court it is essential

Fig. 43 The drop shot (iii) – the follow through

Fig. 44 The backhand dropshot – striking the ball

33

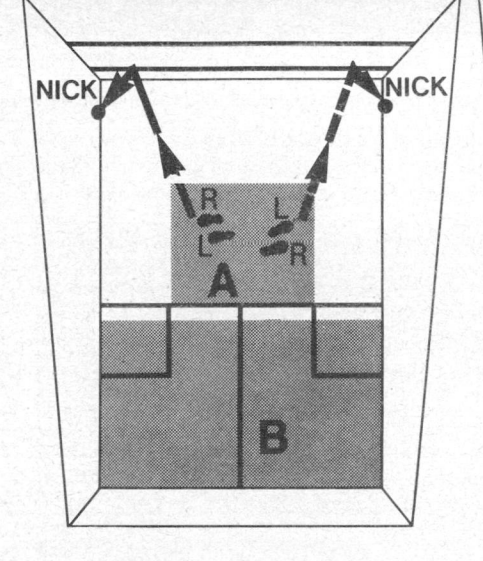

Fig. 45

The most effective drop shots are played in the shaded area "A". Drop shots may be played from poor length shots from area "B," especially against a slow opponent or one who watches the front wall and not the ball when it is behind him.

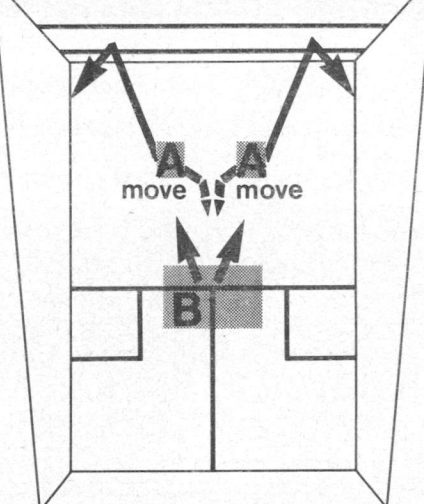

Fig. 46

After a drop shot is played in the front of the court, move away to allow your opponent a fair view.

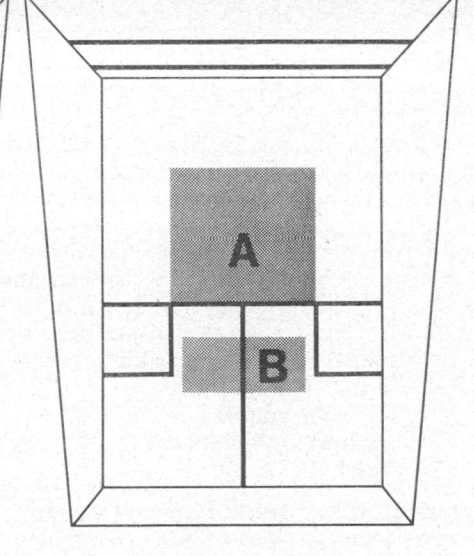

Fig. 47

When the ball is dropping in sector "A," your opponent will usually be somewhere in sector "B," A drop shot should therefore be played.

to move away after completing the stroke to enable your opponent to have a clear view of the ball and to be able to strike it.

For drop shots you must get your left foot well forward and your body well down on the forehand, and your right foot well forward and your body well down on the backhand (this applies to right-handed players).

The best method of practising the drop shot is to start close to the front wall near the centre of the court. Tap the ball gently on to the front wall and then position yourself for the stroke and play it into one of the front corners. When you are satisfied that your footwork is correct and that you are striking the ball correctly, both early and late, then move further and further back in the court until you can play the stroke on to the front wall low down and softly from positions on a level with the service boxes.

Never play a drop shot unless your opponent is behind you, i.e., he must be further back in the court than you are when you strike the ball (Figs. 47 and 48), except for the surprise drop shot from the back of the court off the bad length shot.

To deceive your opponent, take your racket well back before playing the drop shot. This causes a doubt in the mind of your opponent for, if you swing your racket well back, he does not know if a drop shot is about to be played or whether you intend to hit the ball hard to the back of the court, and indeed you can do this at the last moment if you hear him coming up the court having anticipated a drop shot.

The back swing of the racket for the drop shot and for all strokes played in the forecourt is shown in Fig. 41.

Two plans for consideration

PLAN ONE (see Fig. 51).
You can usually tell when your opponent is about to play the drop shot, for he generally places one foot well forward and he crouches a little. Similarly your opponent knows when you are going to play your drop shot. It follows therefore that, except when you play the perfect stroke, your opponent will be able to reach your drop. Now if you play a number of drops you will find that every time you gain a position in front of your opponent he will expect you to play one. You will, therefore, have enticed him up the court, close behind you as you play the stroke. Now, with your full back swing of the racket, you can either hit the ball hard to the back of the court or lob it gently to the back of the court, whichever you please.

PLAN TWO (see Figs. 50 and 51).
Another method of playing the drop shot is to keep very upright as you approach the ball, making it appear that you are going to hit the ball to the back of the court. At the last second you bend down or crouch and you play a drop shot. This is very difficult and needs perfect timing and a great deal of practice. You must watch the ball very closely for this stroke.

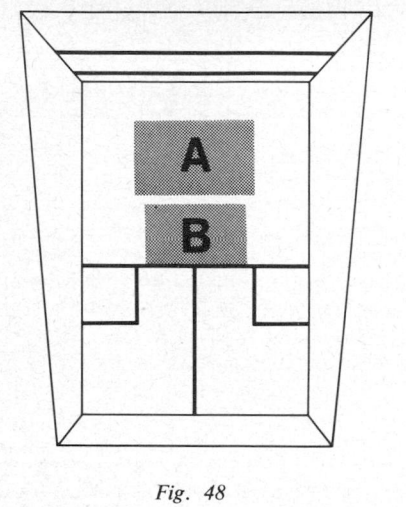

Fig. 48

When the ball is dropping further up the court (in sector "A"), your opponent will usually be in sector "B". A drop shot can be played but a hard-hit drive to the back of the court is probably the best stroke.

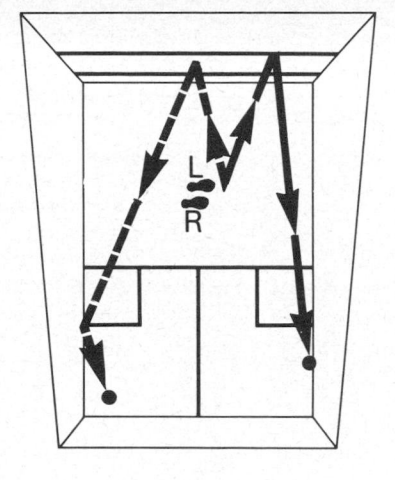

Fig. 49

Hitting the ball into the back of the court (see Plan 1)

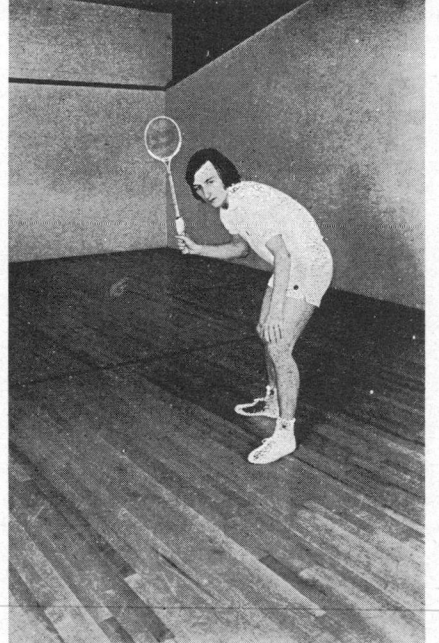

Fig. 50

The back lift position for the deceptive drop shot.

Fig. 50 shows the position when the ball is only two yards away from the player. Could his opponent tell that a drop is about to be played?

Fig. 51 Playing the ball for the deceptive drop shot

THE ANGLE SHOT

The angle shot is one that first hits the side wall and then the front wall. In most cases the ball should be hit hard.

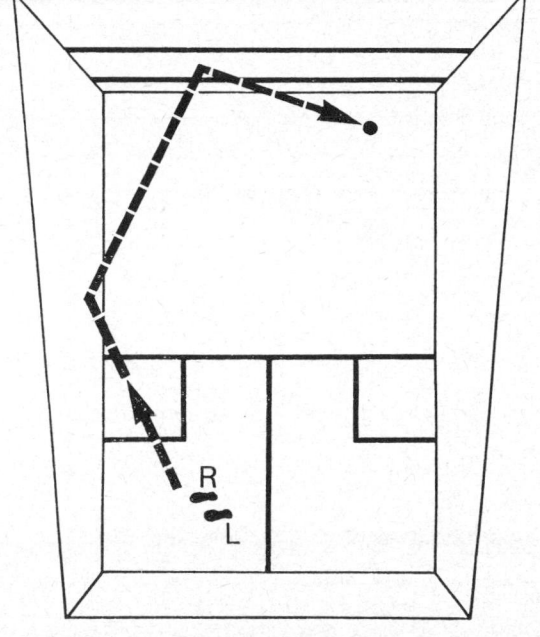

Fig. 52

The angle shot: (i) played from deep back in the court (backhand)

When you strike the ball on the forehand, the left foot is as usual placed well forward and the left shoulder is well round towards the side wall. Similarly, when you strike the ball on the backhand, the right foot is well forward and the right shoulder is well round, pointing at the side wall.

Many players strike the ball very late, well after it has reached the top of its bounce. The best players, when they make winners, play the ball a few inches from the

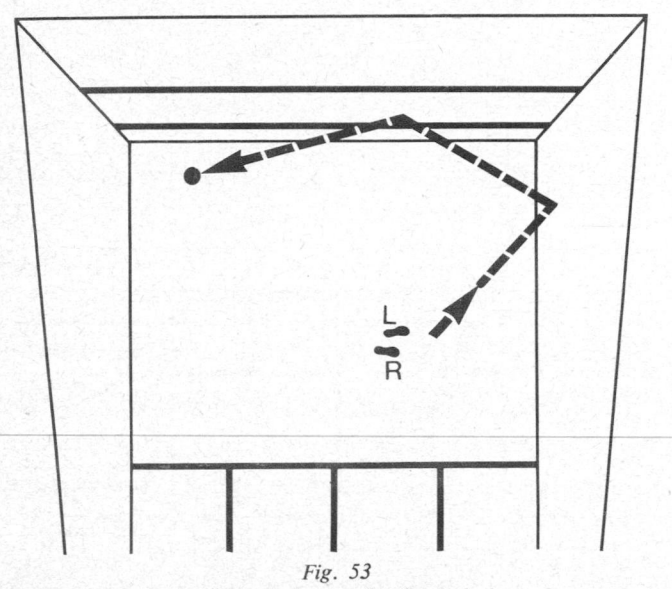

Fig. 53
The best position for the angle shot: (ii) played from in front of the centre line (forehand)

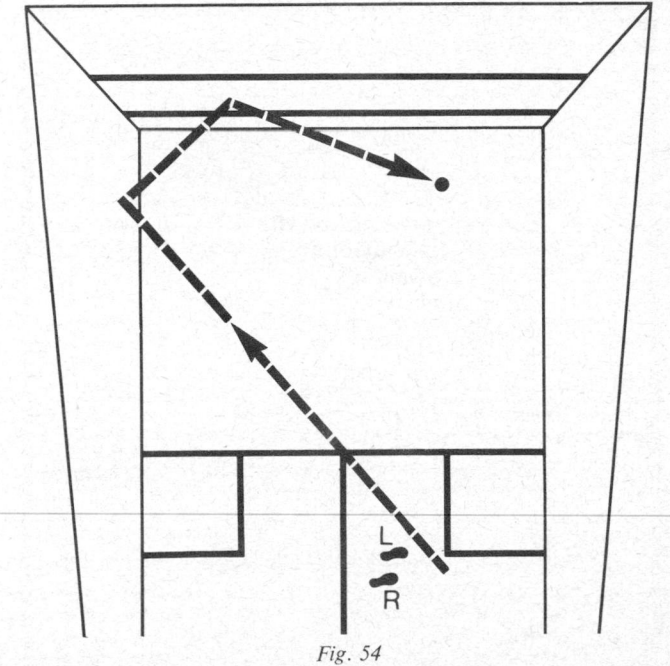

Fig. 54

The reverse angle shot played on the forehand, frequently more effective when played in the front of the court

ground and yet, in the rallies, they often take the ball earlier, before the top of its bounce. This is in order to speed up the game, to make their opponents run and so to tire them. It is indeed most exhausting to be made to move up and down the court. It is far less tiring to run from side to side.

The best positions for the angle shots are shown in Figs. 52 and 53.

The reverse angle stroke is one played on to the opposite side wall (Fig. 54). If played very occasionally it may be a winning stroke, but it is difficult to play accurately.

Do not play an angle shot unless your opponent is either behind you or on a level with you. The only exception to this is when your opponent is moving from the front of the court towards the centre-court position: then you can play an angle or a drop shot. Very often you will catch him completely on the wrong foot.

A match between two really good players may well last up to two hours. The best way for you to tire your opponent is to make him move up and down the court and the best method of doing this is by means of the angle shot. Practise taking the angle shot on the rise and early, for this speeds up the game and your opponent is made to move faster up the court.

Two tactical plans for consideration

PLAN ONE

Masking your strokes is a most important factor in squash rackets. A player often finds himself playing a stroke on his forehand from a position fairly far back in the court.

The position in the court and the stroke for plan one is shown in Fig. 55.

The usual stroke in this case is to hit the ball up the forehand side wall and back into the back corner. Now if you place your shoulder further round towards the side wall and make a full swing of the racket you can take the ball late, and play an angle shot. You must hit the ball hard and play it late.

Equally effective is the same stroke played from deep back on the court on the back hand.

PLAN TWO

This is very similar, but the strokes are played in the front of the court.

During a rally you very often find yourself playing a stroke well up the court on the forehand. From this position you usually play either a drop shot or hit the ball hard to the back of the court.

The position in the court and the stroke for plan two are shown in Fig. 53.

Now by placing your left shoulder further round towards the side wall you can play this quick little angle shot, but you must take a full swing of the racket and must play the ball late.

Equally effective is the same stroke played from well up the court on the backhand.

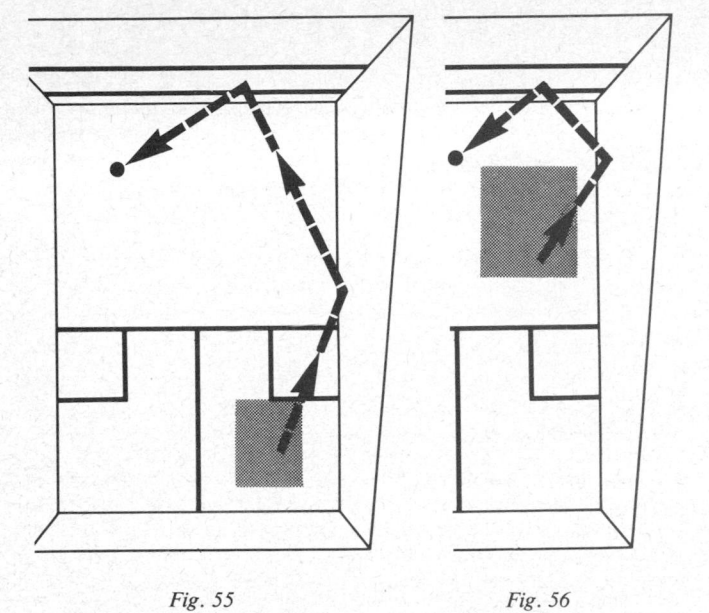

Fig. 55

The shaded area indicates where plan 1, on page 39, can be put into operation

Fig. 56

The shaded area shows where you can strike the ball for plan 2 (see page 39)

VOLLEYING

To be a very good player it is necessary to be a good volleyer. One of the reasons for keeping the head of the racket "up" as you are moving about the court is that this is the easiest position from which to volley. If your racket is trailing near the ground, you will not be able to get it up in time (Fig. 57). No trailer of the racket is ever a good volleyer.

If you ever play against a person who trails his racket you should occasionally hit the ball hard down the centre of the court, *i.e.*, at him as he stands in the centre of the court. You will find that you will be able to make quite a number of winners by this method.

(*a*) Learn to volley the service. You will find that you will not be able to return a slow lob service if you leave it to hit the back wall. In this case volley it close to the side wall, or between the side wall and the back wall.

(*b*) Learn to volley from the centre of the court (Fig. 58).

A great many winners can be made from here. The easiest winner is the quickly played volley, just above the tin, when your opponent is well out of position behind you.

A player who is very fast on his feet can even intercept a cross-court drive from as far forward as the cross on Fig. 58.

Remember that the more you can volley, the more you can speed up the game and you will also save yourself a great deal of running.

(c) To practise volleying, stand in the centre court position and hit the ball hard and high, back at yourself. You will find that you can make winners just above the tin when the ball is about waist or shoulder high.

Remember this and do not try to make winning strokes when the ball is high above your head or low near your feet.

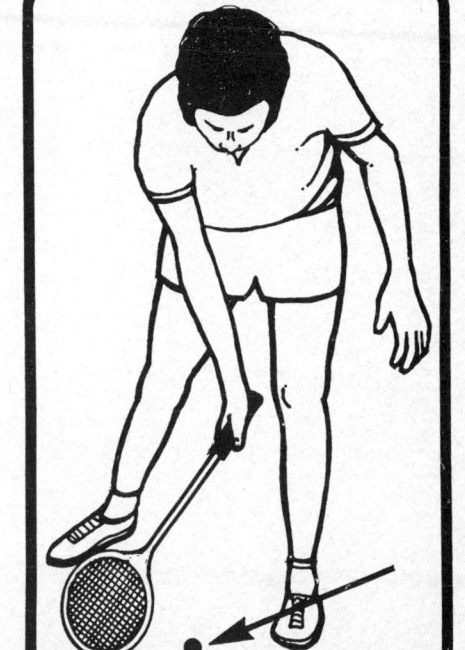

Fig. 59 Playing the half-volley shot

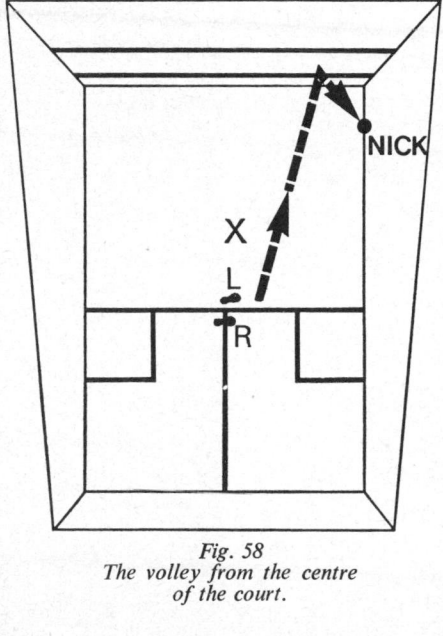

Fig. 58
The volley from the centre
of the court.

Fig. 57
A bad position - never "trail" your racket

41

HALF-VOLLEYING

To half-volley a ball a player must hit it simultaneously with its striking the floor (Fig. 59, page 41).

This is an effective stroke, especially the half-volley drop.

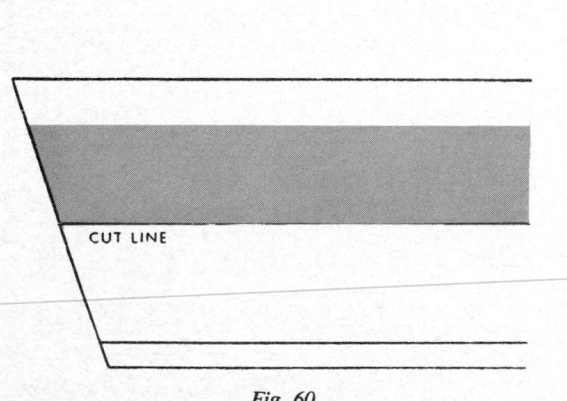

CUT LINE

Fig. 60
The shaded area indicates where the lob shot usually hits the front wall.

Fig. 61 When playing the lob shot, hit the ball at waist level or below and follow through upwards with a good high follow through

LOBBING

This stroke can be one of the most important in the game, either in defence or attack. In defence it enables the striker to recover his position on the "T" before his opponent can play his stroke and in attack it can be devastating when played accurately and to a length, especially on a cold court. The points to note are as follows:

(*a*) the ball can be struck from anywhere in the court.

(*b*) the ball is hit upwards and it is hit only hard enough for it to reach one of the two back corners. Therefore the ball is usually struck when it is either level with your waist or below it.

(*c*) The ball will usually hit the front wall above the cut line. The only exception to this will be when the player is attempting a lob from a position close to the front wall.

The usual position for the ball to hit the front wall is shown in Fig. 60.

(*d*) The ball must pass over your opponent's head as he stands in the centre of the court.

(*e*) The lob can be played most effectively across court, but in either case the ball should strike the side wall and bounce before reaching the back wall, and will thus rebound very little from it.

You cannot smash a good high lob as you can at lawn tennis, and you cannot let it drop into the back corners behind you, so the only effective answer is to volley it defensively. If the ball is within easy reach of your outstretched arm, then it is a bad lob and can be smashed hard, but otherwise volley your return into the back of the court

CHANGE OF PACE

You should try to hit the ball as hard as you can with accuracy and regard this as your "standard pace." Then you can start practising variations of pace. In the rallies you should occasionally play a stroke that is not hit as hard as your standard pace, and occasionally you should hit the ball harder than your standard pace. This change of pace can be very disconcerting to an opponent.

It is most important to disguise this change of pace. Therefore you must take exactly the same back swing and the same follow-through and only accelerate the pace of the racket just before the moment of impact. Similarly, to hit a slower stroke you must take the same back swing and follow-through, but you must slow down the pace of the racket just before the impact.

Now for another aspect of a change of pace. Remember than an opponent may not like the game played at a very fast pace or on the other hand he may not like the game played at a slow pace. Therefore, if you can, you must find out before the end of the first game whether your opponent is vulnerable to a fast or to a slow pace. When you have warmed up and are playing with some accuracy you should increase the pace for a few rallies by hitting the ball harder, taking the ball earlier and volleying more. If this is successful you should continue with it. If not, you should try to slow the game down by hitting the ball later, lobbing more and volleying less.

All this is not as easy as it sounds for, if your opponent

is an experienced player, he is probably trying to do the same thing. If this occurs, then the player who has the greater accuracy will impose his game on the other.

ATTACK AND DEFENCE

All the best players for the last thirty years have made remarkably few mistakes. They have played "perfect" shots close to the tin only when they have had plenty of time to make the strokes. They have realised that by speed about the court and anticipation it is possible to return almost everything. They know that it is unwise to try anything spectacular. It almost seems as if every shot that they play comes either under the heading of a defensive stroke or an attacking one. An attacking stroke would mean a stroke to a length or an attempt at a "perfect" drop or an angle shot played early or very late. A defensive stroke would mean getting the ball up in such a way as to give them time to get to the centre of the court, before their opponent has time to strike the ball.

Stop yourself from trying to make attacking strokes from difficult positions and so avoid making too many errors. To do this get into the habit of saying to yourself as you run for every stroke, "Attack," if you consider that it is going to be an easy shot, or "Defence" if you realise it is going to be a difficult return.

After a time you will find that this process is becoming automatic and resulting in fewer mistakes.

Do not forget that the best defensive stroke is a high one hit slowly. This gives you time to reach the centre of the court. Then, wherever your opponent may hit the ball, you will have a chance to return it.

THE PATTERN OF A RALLY

Most club players and very many county players lack continued concentration. They play well for a few minutes and then they make a succession of foolish mistakes, due entirely to lack of concentration.

You should learn to concentrate throughout every rally, and then to relax, and then to concentrate again for the next rally. This relaxation between the rallies is important. When a rally is finished, forget about it and relax.

Expect every rally to be a long one and realise that the objective is to keep a better length than your opponent. Sooner or later you will get a stroke to the back of the court of such a perfect length that your opponent will either not be able to return it or, if he does, you will be in a position to play an attacking stroke, probably a drop or an angle or a fast stroke down one of the side walls.

This should be what you expect the pattern of every rally to be.

THE DANGER AREA

If you watch a match between two good county players, you will find that out of every ten balls that a player hits down, about five of these errors are made in the danger area shown in Fig. 62.

A drop shot has been attempted in this area and the ball has hit the tin; a lob that was too high above the player's head has been smashed on to the tin; an angle shot has hit the tin. This is an area from which angle shots should be played, so that the opponent can be made to move up the court, but nevertheless angle shots do tend to hit the tin quite often.

If you watch a match between two moderate club players, you will be very surprised to find that out of every ten balls hit down about seven of these errors are made in the danger area.

Surely here is a lesson to be learnt, and it is:

(a) never play a drop shot in the danger area;
(b) only volley defensively in this area;
(c) only play an angle shot in this area when you have plenty of time to get into position for the stroke;
(d) never play a half-volley in this area.

Further back in the court a player takes more trouble to play defensively and far fewer errors are made.

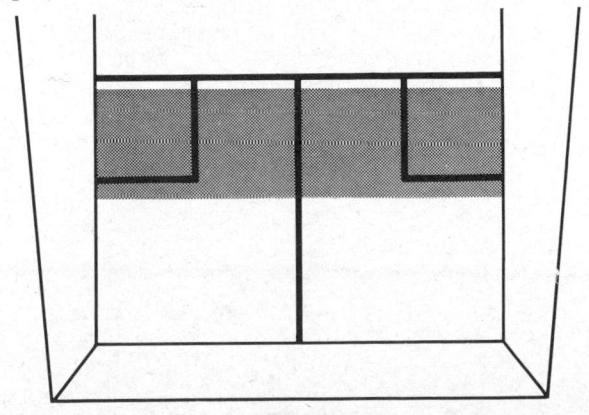

Fig. 62
The Danger area

SELECTED S.R.A. RULES

APPENDIX 1

Rule 4. FAULT

(e) A service is a fault:

(i) if at the time of striking the ball the server fails to have at least one foot in contact with the floor within the service box, and no part of that foot touching the line surrounding the service box (called a foot-fault).

(ii) if the ball is served on to or below the cut line.

(iii) if the ball first touches the floor on or outside the short or half court lines delimiting the back quarter of the court required in Rule 4(c).

(iv) any combination of faults in the one service counts only as one fault.

APPENDIX 2

Rule 8. STROKES, HOW WON

A player wins a stroke:

(a) Under Rule 4(f).

(b) If the opponent fails to make a good return of the ball in play.

(c) If the ball in play touches his opponent or anything he wears or carries, except as is otherwise provided by Rules 9, 10 and 13(a)(i).

(d) If a stroke is awarded by the Referee as provided for in the Rules.

APPENDIX 3

Rule 9. HITTING AN OPPONENT WITH THE BALL

If an otherwise good return of the ball has been made, but before reaching the front wall it hits the striker's opponent, or his racket, or anything he wears or carries, then:

(a) If the ball would have made a good return, and would have struck the front wall without first touching any other wall, the striker shall win the stroke, except if the striker shall have followed the ball round, and so turned, or shall have allowed the ball to pass behind his body, in either case taking the ball on the forehand in the backhand side of the court or vice versa, a Let shall be allowed.

(b) If the ball would otherwise have made a good return, a Let shall be allowed unless, in the Referee's opinion, a winning stroke has been intercepted, then the striker shall win the stroke.

(c) If the ball would not have made a good return, the striker shall lose the stroke. The ball shall cease to be in play, even if it subsequently goes up.

APPENDIX 4

Rule 12. FAIR VIEW, FREEDOM TO PLAY THE BALL, AND INTERFERENCE

(a) After playing a ball, a player must make every effort to get out of his opponent's way. That is:

   (i) a player must make every effort to give his opponent a fair view of the ball, so that he may sight it adequately for the purpose of playing it.

   (ii) a player must make every effort not to interfere with, or crowd, his opponent in the latter's attempt to get to, or play, the ball.

   (iii) a player must make every effort to allow his opponent, as far as the latter's position permits, freedom to play the ball directly to the front wall, or side walls near the front wall.

(b) If any such form of interference has occurred, and, in the opinion of the Referee the player has not made every effort to avoid causing it, the Referee shall on appeal, or stopping play without waiting for an appeal, award the Stroke to his opponent.

(c) However, if interference has occurred, but in the opinion of the Referee the player has made every effort to avoid causing it, the Referee shall on appeal, or stopping play without waiting for an appeal, award a Let, except that if his opponent is prevented from making a winning return by such interference or by distraction from the player, the Referee shall award the Stroke to the opponent.

(d) When, in the opinion of the Referee, a player refrains from playing the ball, which, if played, would clearly and undoubtedly have won the rally under the terms of Rule 9(a) or (b), he shall be awarded the Stroke.

(e) If either the striker or non-striker makes unnecessary physical contact with his opponent the Referee may stop play and award a stroke accordingly.

NOTE TO REFEREES

(i) The practice of impeding an opponent in his efforts to play the ball by crowding or obscuring his view is highly detrimental to the game. Unnecessary physical contact is also detrimental as well as being dangerous. Referees should have no hesitation in enforcing Rule 12(b) and 12(e) above.

(ii) The words "interfere with" in Rule 12(a)(ii) must be interpreted to include the case of a player having to wait for an excessive swing of his opponent's racket.

46

APPENDIX 5

Rule 12. LET, WHEN ALLOWED

Notwithstanding anything contained in these Rules, and provided always that the striker could have made a good return:

(a) A Let may be allowed:

(i) if, owing to the position of the striker, his opponent is unable to avoid being touched by the ball before the return is made.

NOTE TO REFEREES

This Rule shall be construed to include the cases of the striker, whose position in front of his opponent makes it impossible for the latter to see the ball, or who shapes as if to play the ball and changes his mind at the last moment, preferring to take the ball off the back wall, the ball in either case hitting his opponent, who is between the striker and the back wall. This is not, however, to be taken as conflicting in any way with the Referee's duties under Rule 12.

(ii) if the ball in play touches any article lying in the court.

(iii) if the striker refrains from hitting the ball owing to a reasonable fear of injuring his opponent.

(iv) if the striker, in the act of playing the ball, touches his opponent.

(v) if the Referee is asked to decide an appeal and is unable to do so.

(vi) if a player drops his racket, calls out or in any other way distracts his opponent, and the Referee considers that such occurrence has caused the opponent to lose the stroke.

(b) A Let shall be allowed:

(i) if Hand-out is not ready, and does not attempt to take the service.

(ii) if a ball breaks during play.

(iii) if an otherwise good return has been made, but the ball goes out of court on its first bounce.

(iv) as provided for in Rules 9, 10, 11(b)(ii), 18 and 19.

(c) No Let shall be allowed when the player has made an attempt to play the ball except as provided for under Rules 10, 13(a)(iv), 13(b)(ii) and (iii).

(d) Unless an appeal is made by one of the players, no Let shall be allowed except where these Rules definitely provide for a Let, namely Rules 9(a) and (b), 10, 12, 13(b)(ii) and (iii).

APPENDIX 6

Rule 15. KNOCK-UP

(a) Immediately preceding the start of play, the Referee shall allow on the court of play a period not exceeding five minutes to the two players together for the purpose of knocking-up, or in the event of the players electing to knock-up separately, the Referee shall allow the first player a period of $3\frac{1}{2}$ minutes and to his opponent $2\frac{1}{2}$ minutes. In the event of a separate knock-up, the choice of knocking-up first shall be decided by the spin of a racket. The Referee shall allow a further period for the players to warm the ball up if the match is being resumed after a considerable delay.

(b) Where a new ball has been substituted under Rules 13(b)(ii) or 14, the Referee shall allow the ball to be knocked-up to playing condition. Play shall resume on the direction of the Referee, or prior mutual consent of the players.

(c) Between games the ball shall remain on the floor of the court in view and knocking-up shall not be permitted except by mutual consent of the players.

APPENDIX 7

Rule 20.

Players are required to wear white clothing. The referee's decision thereon is final.

The S.R.A. Handbook, obtainable from the Secretary of the Association contains the complete rules. *See overleaf.*

Printed in Great Britain by Sunstreet Printers Keighley, Ltd.

THE SQUASH RACKETS ASSOCIATION'S HANDBOOK

CONTAINS

the complete rules of the game, both singles and doubles; a list of affiliated clubs; records of all the major championships; reports of the previous season; articles of general and historical interest.

from

The General Secretary, The S.R.A.. 70 Brompton Road, London SW3 1DX

Cost: £3.95 plus postage